RIVERS OF REVERIE

MANVI MEHTA

INDIA • SINGAPORE • MALAYSIA

To Grandparents

CONTENTS

PREFACE

A young curious mind, who wrote her first poem at the age of six and loved to play with words and weave them into poetry, begins her journey as a poet with faith as well as apprehension. Now, a woman of experience attempts to write in a genre close to her heart and soul.

Rivers of Reverie is a product of that childhood dream to become a poet. Being the second collection of poems after publishing the first Illuminating The Dawn, this collection attempts to reach all poetry enthusiasts. The poems are on a myriad of themes and will be a home for the heart of the ones, who love to celebrate the written word.

ACKNOWLEDGEMENT

Gratitude is the greatest jewel and I value it the most. To be grateful is to be thankful for all the opportunities and challenges that life offers you in all its phases.

To have the gift of writing is a blessing from the Goddess Durga whom I will be indebted forever.

I extend my heartfelt gratitude to all the readers, who appreciated my first collection of poems Illuminating The Dawn.

I am grateful to my family, teachers, and friends, who have supported me throughout this challenging yet beautiful journey full of exploration.

Manvi Mehta

THE RIVER OF TIME

Originates in the womb of nature,

flows eternally,

Past, Present, Future

we call it differently,

essentially, the same

matter of moments,

pieces of enigma,

yet to fully unravel,

yet to fully comprehend.

REVERIE

Oft in wonder, oft in reverie.

Oft in seeking, the meaning of being

existence begins and how

existence ceases, and why?

Oft I ponder, oft I dream

in trance and moments of tranquillity,

oft I pour words,

oft I pour wisdom inadvertently,

oft I am drunk on words for the relief.

NEW DAWN

The new dawn has arisen with a ray of hope and sunshine,

to brighten the gloomy dull days of yesteryears,

to awaken that dormant mind,

to awaken the soul that is in slumber,

the new dawn has arisen,

with a bright morn in its heart!

WOMAN, THY NAME IS HUMANITY

Frailty, thy name is woman!

Woman, thy name is frailty

they say, I say no!

Thy name is strength and wisdom,

thy character nothing but virtue,

for thy love knows no bounds,

thy strength no limits, thy passion no coyness.

thy word is enough to run a home and a nation,

thy wisdom is enough to quench the curiosity

in anonymity, thy may live yet ignite a thousand minds.
Woman, thy name is humanity!

DEATH

Invitation slipped by,

Death stood staring at me, as if the Oracle had blown its trumpet,

as if the fire was ready to consume me,

as if the earth was ready to embrace me,

an invitation I declined.

Death stared at me,

I stared back into its very eyes,

in its very presence,

neither I begged, nor did I plead.

I was drunk on life, and that I declared.

I fought and fiercely fought against destiny,

against fate,

against odds,

I emerged stronger and

I murdered death.

MIRROR

Reflections are my essence, beholders are my companion

perspectives, reality and imagination I give back, everything I receive.

Many have aged with me, many have dreamt with me

dreams, truth and lies I consume it all.

Secrets are safe with me, desires are well-kept

fears, freedom and boundaries I receive it all.

Thousand broken pieces still have a way of showing paths,

thousand broken pieces, still have a way of giving life.

AMIDST

Amidst the lost yesterdays and unborn tomorrows,

in the embrace of today,

I looked at you and time suddenly froze.

Amidst the clouds, and the moonlight
in the sunshine,

I dreamt about you and the seasons changed.

Amidst the hopes and the despair
in the moment of chance,

I found you and the universe conspired.

A CONSCIOUS MANDATE

The nation wrapped in the night of darkness,

The nation is on the verge of losing its glory,

The nation in the conflict between right and wrong,

The nation burning in the fire of ignorance,

The nation that longs for a saviour.

A saviour who restores, the fine balance between rights and duties.

Where is the nation of my dreams?

Look no forward than a mirror,

The saviour is you; the saviour is I,

The saviour is us.

So, the mandate must reflect this.

So, the representation must reflect this.

The power is with us.

One vote can change the health of the economy,

One conscious vote can be the beginning of a new era, in India.

IF WORDS HAD WINGS

If words had wings,

they would fly from the window of my heart to yours.

Whisper the well-kept secret

stories of unabashed emotions,

if words had wings.

They would perch on your soul and sing the most melodious songs,

but only if words had wings.

Then one day, I realised words do have wings,

they fly from the window of one heart to another.

And give hope and solace like an oasis in the dreary desert.

Yes, words do have wings you merely need to give them a try.

PERIOD

A drop of blood and the skirt was shamed, the girl became a woman but impure, she was named

excluded from the kitchen and touching the pickle,

that was the patriarchal set-up and was to belittle,

the womanhood that should have been celebrated was termed impurity.

Are we still evolving as a society?

BIRTH

I looked in the mirror, the scars looked beautiful today,

for the tales of fear and faith were embedded in each of them,

the screams and the horror amid bloodshed amid terror, I was still living.

Death lured me, but I didn't succumb.

I took a breath and the story of a new life began.

LOVE IS LOVE

The pandemic hit them hard, life changed in a heartbeat. She was far in lockdown in another city, she too was far

but sick, not just with the pandemic but sick with the world.

that had not accepted their kind of love.

But love is love, they both said and defied the societal set-up, defied the normal that was conformity but, love is the love they told each other

with distance, but a heavyweight on their souls with time but consuming them both.

In a world of fiction, these characters lived in a world of reality, she and her lover were named called

conforming to the societal set-up, ruined their souls.

They instantly understood,

that the world was not ready for their love,

with just a narrow definition of love,

the societal set-up was blind,

the societal set-up was behind

humanity was nowhere to be found

the love of the same sex lived,

but somewhere they both died.

ON MOTHERHOOD

A damaged heart,

a damaged soul

wings broken

alone

resists the sky, for it fears, the fall

resists the night, for it fears, the dark

resists the dawn, for it fears, the sun,

the scorching heat

the ray that pierces its soul.

But for the sake of motherhood,

braves it all,

to feed its young ones,

dares to fly

broken maybe, the wings

but spirits high.

NATURE

When the sun comes up, we can tell a new lie.

We can weave a new story,

with each ray escaping the mundane and the ordinary.

We can light up our worlds with the new dawn.

We can fabricate a tale never heard of.

And when the sun sets, and the dusk sets in we can choose.

Choose to be in the world, we wove for ourselves or get trapped in the reality.

Then again, when the sun comes up,

with raindrops as our ink and the leaves as our paper.

We can write nature's eternal blessings in our lives.

MIRACLE

An island rose from the sea -

Like an oasis in the dreary desert,

Like a ray of sun on a gloomy day,

Like spring that follows the snow.

Waking from a slumber,

When faith opened its eyes,

Prayers were answered.

Amidst the brutality,

Amidst the innate animalistic instincts of humankind.

And the fury of nature,

Miracle happened.

And the island gave shelter to the drowning lives.

WORDS

Brevity is the soul of wit.

Wit, the soul of words

For words can pierce or purge,

For words can heal or consume.

Like a candle or fire,

Like the very Sun that shines to brighten but can very much melt this too, too, solid flesh.

RENDEZVOUS

Where the night envelopes the sun, where the moon outshines the stars, where the ocean swallows the land, where volcanoes turn everything to ashes; there - you and I – shall meet!

CUT FROM REALITY

Under the sky filled with scintillating stars,

In the cool breeze of a winter night, She met a stranger.

It was as if the universe conspired,

And they were meant to be a part of each other's lives.

With endless laughter and tears,

With a mixed bag of emotions. They fit into each other's lives, like pieces of a puzzle.

They were alike yet different.

Poles apart yet connected with the thread of fate.

The connection they felt was different.

The connection they felt was unique.

Like roses and thorns,

Like day and night,

Like light and darkness.

But one day, she realized that the stranger was nothing but a figment of her imagination.

Had no existence beyond the world of her mind.

She was cut from reality,

She was in hallucination,

Everyone labelled her insane.

Yes, she was different indeed she was different.

But not in the way the world perceived her.

Not in the way the world gossiped about her.

She was in pain,

She was suffering,

Cut from reality.

She was in hallucination,

She could still hear whispers.

She could still sense the soul mate near her.

But only solace, her soul mate was nothing but imagination.

Alas, her condition deteriorated.

Alas, she was diagnosed with Schizophrenia.

A much less known mental disorder,

Cut from reality.

She was in pain,

Her suffering was unbearable.

Her pain was intolerable.

She cut herself to get rid of it all,

Blood flowed like a river of emotions.

She thought she would be at peace,

But she could not escape the reality of her being in imagination.

She was in hallucination,

Cut from reality.

On the verge of losing sanity,

To quote Shakespeare:

The dilemma of "to be or not to be."

She was one in a thousand.

She was a representative of the thousands suffering from this disorder.

She was the chosen one. Then, she was lying on her deathbed.

Braving it all.

The next morning, brought the message of death Imagination and reality merged.

Blurred faces.

Blurred memories.

Everything was in unison.

Few came by to bid her a final goodbye.

With flowers and words of love,

Which she longed for all her life.

Few came by to bid her a final goodbye.

On her grave, they carved the words,

"You were one amongst us,

You lived a life less ordinary,

You were different and rare,

May you eternally be at peace."

Her story struck a chord with me, for I too live a similar life.

Maybe not the degree of her pain.

Maybe not the degree of her suffering.

But I too am vulnerable.

They say I am rare,

They say I am different,

But they seldom ask me, why?

But seldom want to know, why?

ON POETRY

Darkness doesn't haunt me anymore,

In the quilts of dreams, I write.

Void of any reason,

Save that of ink,

With blood and a bit of ink.

Mincing no words I declare,

Poet at heart I am.

My emotions consummate with words.

Poetry, their offspring.

ASHES

Thou loved me fiercely once,

Now have forgotten.

The letters of love,

The moments of passion.

Thou called me thy life once,

Now want no glimpse of me.

Thou kept my portrait in thy heart.

Now ashes are where, it sleeps.

ON LOSS

Slumber lost its spell on me,

sleepless nights I have spent.

Sceptical of what lies ahead of me, lost not just love but a piece of me.

The heart does beat yet numb.

Yes, alive I stood looking at the pyre

staring at the fire.

Consume not just the dead but a part of me.

Yes, alive I stood in ashes, searching for a part of me.

FRAGRANCE OF YOU

In quietude and solitude,

I find myself a mirror of you.

Pieces of me reflect parts of you,

In the hustle-bustle and noise of the city.

I find myself a shadow of you,

Clad in your colour, I reflect the character of you.

You and I,

I and You.

In the maze of life,

Look for each other in the ink that spells words.

In the blood that spells love,

In the eyes that spin a tale,

In the old books and the memories,

Handwritten letters are still kept safe.

Roses dried and died yet precious,

In the petals and letters.

I still find the fragrance of you.

COURAGE

Braving it all with a smile, inner battles that none know of. Standing against the test of time, fighting your demons. Standing against all odds.

Isn't it a reflection of the strength of character? Isn't it a reflection of courage and conviction in facing your fears?

When the odds of winning are minimal, still endure.

When the road is full of obstacles, still walking. This is power and strength.

Don't think so?

Then, it is time to contemplate again.

SELF LOVE

Dear me,

Saying that I love you would be an understatement

for I adore you, respect you and

mostly, am in awe of you

being with you is not only the reason that I am in love with you,

but it is also you being you that makes you unique and special,

and that makes me fall in love with you all over again, you are my pride my reason to be inspired, I must tell you how amazing you are not for your looks or status, but your gracious heart.

ENDURANCE

Delusions and fragmented thoughts,

Mid-night conversations,

With none but self.

Meaningless and sleepless nights,

The reminder of the ticking clock,

The reminder to be alright,

Amid anxiety and fright.

The voices in the head

Endure, endure, endure!

Echoes the night,

Solace is the lap, where I want to rest.

Peace is the lullaby a want to hear.

Ah! One more window broken.

Ah! one more home shattered.

Prison is where I live

Amid the horror of the unsafe streets.

Amid the screams,

Amid the atrocities,

Then an echo again

Endure, endure, endure!

I murmur

Until when?

DARK TRUTH

The fire within you, ignites the passion within me.

Your heart, beats to the rhythm of my name.

my heart races to your smile.

Modern love is such that you are someone's, I am someone's But our hearts crave to beat for each other. Maybe someday, maybe in some moment of truth, this dark secret will reveal itself.

MERGE

Eyes that behold at the sparkle of your eyes, love that craves the same from your side, seeking beyond you is seeking beyond myself,

I am the river, whose ripples chant your name, be the ocean and merge me within.

EMBERS

Dying embers of love,

Dying embers of friendship, once lovers in the sand of time, now fading memories is that I find.

Dying embers,

Fading glimpse,

Of you and me.

Of beginning and end.

Of chapters incomplete unwritten and unspoken of,

Wilting flowers of the autumn I see, remind me of season and changes. But till when will I wait for the Spring?

ENNUI

Filled me a cup of tea, filled me a chance again. To live and to flourish.

But ennui is I am succumbing to,

Ennui haunts me during the day.

It bothers me at the night,

Of life and death.

And death and life,

Slices of happiness, I seek slices of peace in the trauma of my mind.

Ennui I shake hands with,

Death I make peace with,

Corpse you will call me, I call liberation from the prison of the body.

Ennui and I are inseparable,

Walking the path into the dark and unknown.

Ignorance is bliss at times,

Ennui whispers and I quit life.

AFTERMATH

Woke up from a nightmare,

My soul is still in shivers.

The destruction I saw was colossal,

The aftermath is unbearable.

The collapse of civilization in a minute,

Animalistic instincts have crept in again.

Apocalypse is near,

Apocalypse is arriving,

Hope has lost its charm,

Faith is drowned somewhere.

Ushering the end,

Ushering the damage,

Madness is the new regime.

Cannot foresee anything but the bloodbath,

And our hands filled with the murder.

Chaos, bloodshed, and disorder.

Either I will succumb to all this,

Or my soul will be pulled out barbarically.

The aftermath is just the beginning of the end,

The end is coming with the speed of light. Will we survive it by any means?

ELEMENT

In my element,

In my place,

I often wonder about the vacant space,

Where seeds I once planted are trees with ripened fruits now.

In my element,

In my inner secret safe,

Dried flowers I kept.

For those were precious,

Are still spreading fragrance.

In my element,

In my dreams,

In the night sky,

I eloped once with the shooting star.

In my element,

In my notebook,

I find peace in words,

I once scribbled in madness,

In my element.

The other side of me insane, and screaming

In my element,

The other side is intruding.

EPHEMERAL

Seconds, minutes, hours flowing; like a river, a splash of waves a mystery of time, a minute seems an era, an era seems a second. Tick, tick, tick, echoes the dusk and screams the night.

"Do not sleep until its reality,

do not wake up to the illusion of the ephemeral."

The path, you tread is dark and unknown but do not stop, until you ignite the fire, the passion, the wisdom,

do not settle for the ephemeral pleasure

seek the eternal light.

ABOUT THE AUTHOR

Manvi Mehta, born and brought up in Jaipur, The Pink City of Rajasthan is an Assistant Professor of Economics and a Poet. The author of the collection of poems *Illuminating the Dawn* is passionate about poetry since childhood. Playing with words and weaving them into pearls of poetry has been most satisfying. Her second collection of poems *Rivers of Reverie* gives the readers an emotional ride and makes them contemplate, introspect, and reflect. The poems are relatable and explore complex themes in ways that the readers will have an enriching experience.